A GAZE HOUND THAT HUNTETH BY THE EYE

PITT POETRY SERIES

EDITORS

TERRANCE HAYES
NANCY KRYGOWSKI
JEFFREY MCDANIEL

A GAZE HOUND THAT

A GAZE HOUND THAT
A GAZE HOUND THAT
A GAZE HOUND THAT

A GAZE HOUND THAT

HUNTETH BY THE EYE

HUNTETH BY THE EYE
HUNTETH BY THE EYE
HUNTETH BY THE EYE
HUNTETH BY THE EYE

V. PENELOPE PELIZZON

UNIVERSITY OF PITTSBURGH PRESS

Published by the University of Pittsburgh Press, Pittsburgh, Pa., 15260

Copyright © 2024, V. Penelope Pelizzon

Printed on acid-free paper

10 9 8 7 6 5 4 3 2 1

ISBN 13: 978-0-8229-6721-7
ISBN 10: 0-8229-6721-9

Cover art: Deborah Dancy, *Mapping an Afterthought*, 2020. Oil on canvas, 38 × 34 inches. Courtesy of the artist.
Cover design: Joel W. Coggins

for my familiars

The foreigner allow you to be yourself
by making a foreigner of you.

—EDMOND JABÈS

CONTENTS

A GAZE HOUND THAT HUNTETH BY THE EYE

A GAZE HOUND THAT HUNTETH BY THE EYE

Cf. William Harrison, "Of Our English Dogs and Their Qualities,"
Holinshed's Chronicles, 1587

It's not criminal: it isn't sodomy
    or taking horses to Scotland
        or poaching the king's deer.
      Though it seems like witchcraft, this
entranced spasm of pleasure my presence

triggers in my wriggling pup. Now lap-ensconced,
    she gobbles a fancy kiln-dried
        carp skin, snowing its small
      smelly flakes on the carpet.
Her squid-tentacle tongue slaps my chin—joy!

But this cuddling repels Mister Harrison,
    Vicar of Wimbish. He's gathered
        descriptions of English
      dogs, furniture, fashions, fairs,
sundry corporal punishments and ships

flying her majesty's flag for chronicles
    Shakespeare will pinch from to flesh out
        his kings. If I didn't
      know by now how much I know
sieves down to me from men who winced at dames

soothing their hot spells or chilly wombs with love
    minced into morsels and hand-fed
        to pets, my face would sting
      afresh below the vicar's
volley of slaps. How he despises us,

irksome older women *trifling away all*
　　　　treasure of time with our perverse
　　　　　　cossetings. Some feeble
　　　　palsied ladies even tuck
a little peke or pug inside their shawls

for warmth! Poor man. He's better off dead, not here
　　　　forced to catalogue how, today,
　　　　　　I climbed off my broomstick
　　　　and smooched my leashed familiar
shamelessly on her damp nose, taking her

along to weed my pandemic victory
　　　　garden. Of course, true victory
　　　　　　gardens grow human food;
　　　　my perennials will feed
mainly bees. Call it my foresight garden,

all charms still speculative. Last week I lost
　　　　hours online looking for blue
　　　　　　false indigo, native
　　　　but hard to find this season
of quarantined green thumbs with their itchy

digger-fingers lusting to plug a few dead
　　　　-seeming sticks in dirt. (My vaccine
　　　　　　against panic's fussing
　　　　about how I'm going to set
this smatter of pale blue hearts aflutter

over new beds of hyssop.) Soiled and toil-sore
        from planting, last night I bedded
                King *Richard II*,
            book on my belly in air
    finally warm enough to lie naked

atop the sheets in, windows flung open
        to the spring peepers' rainy bells.
                In Shakespeare's uterus
            of a mind the chronicles
    seeded this fruit. It offered me toothsome

distractions from the news—Richard's a wretched
        leader, but he's not a human
                trashfire like some. Who's fit
            to govern the garden of
    the state? Flinchless, the first Elizabeth

dead-headed traitors and shut plaguey stages
        but she had, I recall, the heart
                and stomach of a man.
            She left no issue but art
    breastfed on the rich milks of empire

her ships ploughed the seas to reach. Settlers came here
        and native people not yet sick
                taught them about dying
            cloth blue with false indigo.
    What hunger for blue! So scarce in nature,

had I myself lived in a warm colony
  farmed by captive labor circa
    1740, I
   too might have owned a rich crop
 of color, breeding wealth. Indigo's stench

poisoned those who boiled and pounded the leaves, but
  back then I might have seen only
    pretty buds. Resilient
   reminder of forced transplants,
 false indigo improves poor soil, as if

blooming is the best revenge. This sprout I've set
  will be a triumphant blue shout
    I'll bow to, salaaming
   as I weed. Blue tints, so rare
 they're absent from this antique kelim, scaled

now with carp skin. The corner's askew, pooch-chewed
  one New Year's eve in New York's fret-
    work of fire-works. Good thing
   the vicar didn't catch me
 next dawn, old bitch crouched beneath a scything

wind off the Gowanus canal, poking through
  my mutt's scat with a plastic straw
    picked out of the gutter
   to make sure the shreds of heir-
 loom vegetable-dyed wool had made a safe

backstage exit. I'd not have the vicar's ilk
       see me bend. No. I kneel only
              in service to new growth
         thickening the history
    of gardens, tending to those I adore.

ORTS & SLARTS

Nothing's less romantic than a dish of lentils
           amped up with ramps and garlic
    turning you into a wind instrument
    sprawled across the couch in torment. Nothing's
          more humorous than an aunt
embarrassed, her innards muttering crass

blasphemies in some guttural proto-Nordic
           dialect. Well, Gassy Lassie,
    none will celebrate your dignity's lapse
    happily as this trio of nephews,
          avid hagiographers
who praise the body's stinks and stews, its anarchy

deflating false modesty. They mythologize
           their seismic eructations
    and erections, regale you with sagas
    of J.'s puss-blister and how D.'s whacked head
          bled and when W. yacked
asparagus in the tub. It's sublime, really,

what fumes to the surface when expert fartisans
           descend to hilarity.
    You'd have an awkward time with politer
    friends who lacked these children's intimacy
          with the rebellious corpus.
Unable much of the fall to hug their father

whose kisses the chemo made radioactive,
           their hero is not a brute
    Hercules dragging his lion-pelt, but

the gaunt man whose eyebrows have just begun
             caterpillaring back, who
spoons pancake batter onto the griddle to birth

their favorite animals. Eggless batter, since
             their systems aggressively
      reject allergens. (What poison came home
      in sippy cup lids or pacifiers?
             With milk in plastic cartons?
Toxins tasteless in the butter-sweet colostrum

warm from the nipple of a mama bear who's breathed
             what breezes off the golf course
      airport highway slaughterhouse mephitic
      sugar refining plant?) An egg mishap,
             unlike a fuck-up with nuts,
might not kill anyone but surely would induce

great bouts of yacking! in the tub! And flatulence,
             a word they can't stop wafting
      in laughter as mom rebukes yet again,
      yanking the pouch from a hand old enough
             to know better—*no cursing*
please; these aren't toys; your EpiPen is not a gun.

THE SOOTE SEASON

Again these mornings where child adductions
appear most visibly in parks, light newly
minting the new leaves. Small white babies
crooked freshly-diapered in the arms
Jamaican ladies offer, babies small and white
milked back to sleep on the bosoms of Russia,
bosoms that farther back in the darkness
Q-lined in from Brighton Beach, having pressed
their own babies into the arms a sister or mother
yawned wide for them on the couch. A green
mantilla of shadow feminizes the park.
Laconic, the dog and I walk, aristocrats
among those who know the names of pets
but meet with shyness another human's look.

Mostly our glances stay low. We socialize
instead with strokes along a proffered jaw,
with compliments for grooming and behavior.
Wordlessly, our awkward treat is taken.
Here, with the utmost pleasure, I've cupped
the tapered chamfer of a greyhound's skull
like a chalice in my palms, and bent to smell
her fur's bouquet, the same flinted floral breath
mown grass exhales in summer. Though I am
a gaze hound that hunteth by the eye, her master
raises his look limply only as far as my chin
before he drops it like a gnawed ball
to roll across the greensward of his screen.
Incarnate time runs past us toward school.

Over their shoulders, yoga-goers hoist mats
rolled cigar-wise in eco-cotton wrappers.
Downward dog. The Ommm of a long exhalation
suspended over the park. Earnest summer
comes bounding, promising its kale-flavored
vape smoke, deluscious apricot slashes
of sunset over Red Hook, bottled water
sourced at far-off fonts with lovely names
and, to cool the unctuous burn of poison ivy
waded through upstate, a Q-tip dipped
in refrigerated calamine then dabbed
between the toes, though I do this now
only for myself, this remembered suburban
gentleness once my mother's province.

What hunger led the first hominid to feed
scarce meat to a wolf and thereby nurture
trust attuned to our every gesture
more fully than we trust our species?
Before he'd rent to me my landlord insisted
we Skype to ascertain, it dawned on me
chatting about the block's amenities,
sycamores, and extreme safety, although
nothing was spoken, that I was a person
sinecured and stable, and unsable.
The apartment is sunny and affordable.
I signed the lease. The dog does his business,
which I scoop in a baggie made for the job.
Around us, nannies gloze their querulous

charges with sugar, such sweetness, a fine glucose
pollen sifting over the beautiful trees.
Nana, three twins! a niblet in pigtails crows
pointing at a stroller with all-terrain wheels
adapted from a NASA rover, awed
as I am by how fecund imagination
grows when given a market, imagination
fluent, almost, as money. One walking
her antique poodle freshly pollarded
can't not notice the nursemaids' apartheid
—Jamaicans on the swings, Eastern Bloc
having commandeered the sandbox—
each stand-in mother's tongue staking out
its turf on the recycled tire surface.

BLUE HOUR

The last late rain-scaled light has swum
along the office wall.
An aggrieved

mosquito-whine of all you've not achieved
needles. But your pen's aphasic.
Each hypnotic tick

of keyboard pecked by finger
only deepens torpor.
Sleep you've skimped

drapes its limp
gauze across your focus.
You yawn, procrastinate,

succumb,
drawn downward
into an abyss

of click-bait,
the screen a lamp
you cannot brush the charred

moths of your attention from.
It's too late for caffeine,
too early for wine, this hour between

dog walk and wolf-whistle,
the daymind and its lunar
eclipse.

Light slips
further into shadow.

Time to go.

Still, spent as you are,
you linger,
meeting in the witness of the window

slowly becoming mirror
an oblique blue
attuned

to failure,
its cold stare reflecting in you
a yearning, intent

though silent,
to be somewhere else, or
someone different.

CALL & RESPONSE

A nervous dog will snap at wind
that snarls outdoors as snows descend
till only walking pacifies
the wolf awoken in the hound.

We trudge the path we've memorized,
our coats first nipped, then gnashed at by
fangs within the sharpened cold,
grown sharper as the daylight dies.

Ice rusts the hinges of the oaks.
Like owls, they screech at us below
& we, forgetting what we are,
flinch beneath that killing blow.

But soon we're swallowed in the roar
streams of rush-hour traffic pour.
Pink neon from the Eastbrook Mall
(our northern lights) erases stars

we know still seethe, invisible,
these nights we feel their anxious pull
deep inside the animal
asleep inside each animal.

ILL-STARRED

Ice. Tree. Your ski pole
jabbed at the wrong sharp angle.
Flung forward, your sprawl

seems slo-mo; you're like
a starfish peeled off its rock
rough hands have tossed back—

terribly free, it
hangs in the air an instant,
twinkling. Then you hit,

hearing a soft crunch.
(Had you descended an inch
closer to the branch

that would've been skull.)
But you don't feel pain; you feel
boneless. The muscle

along the break's edge
is shocked numb; wrecked cartilage
can't sense the damage

yet. Isn't the air
extraordinarily clear?
Nothing is clearer

now to you. As if
cares leashing you to yourself
have snapped, you're let off

the hook. Immediate
problems feel safely remote.
No cold, no thirst, not

fearing the worst—for
you've left no note. Who'll explore
off-route trails after

finding your car? When?
But this compels you less than
the spent sun's design,

azure and freaks of
orpiment slashed by dark mauve
hawk talons above

silhouette pine tops
you can't but admire, hap-
less as your collapse

under them was. Stars
(or is it Venus and Mars?)
rise. Their fire shivers

a little, the way
coins tossed in a fountain pay
out, then snatch away

the gleams their faces
refract up through the nervous
water's kicked surface.

The stars brighten. Or
do they darken? You've piqued their
interest with your

stillness, intriguing
them to lean closer, squinting
to see you, sea-thing,

chill echinoderm
who, in its salt medium,
would regrow that limb.

ELEGY FOR _____

There's no   —what was it?

Cold sparks from the moon
                              Cold flecks of spit
dashed from the wolves' teeth as they surged
down from the north, ice alight in their fur

I caught it on my tongue, calling its falling "like petals"
          "pollen"
                    "pale feathers"
                              "swarms of silver bees"
          "like a jillion glassy minnows aswim in the jar
          of light below the streetlamp"

An old book compared it to grain
hoarded in heaven's storehouse
till its master saith *Be thou on the earth*

(& sometimes it fell slowly, careful as the snippets
dropped by a child's scissors cutting out
its image from a sheet of paper folded into pleats)

Drifts, we named its gatherings
& we piled it up in poems
          on breasts white as
          hands white as

cheeks pale as
building effigies of women for centuries
freezing & thawing thawing & freezing

(but I don't blame it
for all the mouths it melted in)

So did you ever see it?

I saw it many times

You saw it many times?

Many, or once
and once and once and once
each flake "unique" as we liked
saying, tho
what did we mean

was each more singular than any
beetlewing waterdrop dustgrain
magnified   more singular than the merged scintillant
irises of anyone I ever swam into
while kissing

A loveliness that more and more
(or less and less) each winter
stung me   those specks landing for an instant on
a coatsleeve   naked branch   horse's whiskers   the gray
wrinkles of the river
swallowing them   fleeting   as if they'd never been

GYPSY MOTHS

caterpillar stage

A silk mistake, imported for your thread's potential
(the shantung shining in the speculator's eyes)
        since you, unlike your cousin *bombyx*, graze
unfinicky on leaves of every species. Now you nibble
        forests to lace. A silicotic lung
sickens one morning in my oak tree's vast estate.
Its speckles hatch, and soon, by inches, devastate,
        chewing till I walk among
slicks of frass to mourn the branches' skeletons.
        The woods around me rustle with the patter
of countless soft digestive tubes raining fecal matter
        as you profit from distemper in the seasons:
one fungus, finding you delicious, spun through you every spring
        and snipped your threads within, but that
        was back before the weeks of wet
        its spores require to sprout began delaying
arrival while your eggs had not. You curse the deer,
        the nesting birds, the squirrels, all who forage
        acorns or shelter in the foliage.
        You curse the person who can hear
a tree falling before it falls, who loved its leaves,
        on days when the weather was changeable as a mind,
                susurrating in wind
and silvering their silky freshly-woven sleeves.

AFRICA HAND

Put a spacey driver behind the wheel.
        Drop her in the opposite hemisphere.
    Flummox her by juggling the seasons,
fill nights with alien stars, let constellations
       she's memorized appear

downside up… in this reversed world,
      the mirror-hand manual transmission
a sinister contraption, I veer a narrow
line between pedestrians I winnow,
      nearly, and head-on collision.

But there's a trance the road induces. Drive
      long enough, I start wondering how far
crows fly between Limpopo and Zambezi,
wanting to taste again the lambent-fizzy
      ginger beers in Zanzibar,

imagining radio broadcasts of the last
      songs of Songhai. Or Axum's lost maxims
set to music. Or podcasts with the Nok
potters, 200 C.E., addressing their knack
      for figures. *Caller three, Kanem's*

mosque was where? Who made Warka puppets
      dance? Whence the silks in Kawkaw's market?
If only the AmaXhosa had colonized Wessex,
my tongue would mix alveolar clicks
      into the plummy jam of my accent,

though chakalaka to shakshuka, con-
    tinental condiments Cape to Cairo
do spice my tongue… Meanwhile, my handbag (not
in hand, abandoned on the passenger seat),
    sprouts a strap, making it low

hanging fruit for harvest through the open
    window at a stoplight. My takeaway:
what's under your nose is safer under your thumb,
ma'am. The cop doesn't call me dumb;
    his eye-roll does it: your naiveté

is dazzling; white people have their fingers
    stuck in every pie; how come you haven't
learned to keep your hands on your own shit?
And now you're in my station, frit-
    tering my time? This scolding, silent,

conveyed by a ripple as of water
    sluicing over stones, tumbles downward
from his crows' feet, past the grottos of his nostrils,
laps across his lips and, in little rills,
    settles at his chin, so it's hard

not to see he's not unkind. I find
    in Africa there isn't any shortage
of gardens my stupidity can bloom in.
Back home, the dangerous creatures are human.
    Here even the foliage

has teeth. Last week near Lusikisiki,
            I didn't peek before poking a tendril of vine
      lacing a bush where something was causing a fracas
      among birds. Then I saw scales, dark as
                  leaves. And the serpentine

coils of another kingdom. Not vegetable.
            I caught my own reflection in the eye
      watching the fingers I'd grazed along her flank,
      almost. Boomslang. Venom haemotoxic.
                  Bitten, your organs liquefy;

you piss blood, blood rusts your spit. But
            she's shy. My hand slithered back from the abyss
      slowly. Dear gods, dear apotropaic charms, a
      snake in the bush is worth—what? One hamsa,
                  shock-eyed, rich in its emptiness.

ANIMALS & INSTRUMENTS

Avis Dam, Windhoek, Namibia

. . . like baboons barking.

                Like these baboons by the parking lot, females flashing
melon-ripe vaginas. Or the dog who salutes my front tire, sending his fellow smelle
a p-mail with martial subject line—

                    like them, we're brilliant at making signs

furred and clawed . . . furred and clawed
and beaked, our languages

             —so often we've plucked

what tools we sign them with
from other signers' bodies.

        Like feathers.

    •   •   •

It's wild, really,
how fast my students type, how hesitant they are to jot
anything by hand. Look, I tell them, writing sharpens synapses; it helps us
remember dates. Let's keep notes on paper
for the term's last weeks, shall we? So now
it's our class joke: *My little chickadees, take up your quills!*
And birds at recess spur them to trill out *Miss, a pen!*

                  You'd laugh, wouldn't you,
my chickadees, to see me out for a Sunday hike around the lake
led by a one-eared dog, wading through grasses
spiked with newly molted plumes of geese?

               Here's a beauty: long as my fingertips
to wrist twice over, raffishly striped in shark and cream
once I smooth its ziplock barbules . . . A sixteenth-century quill no lovelier

than this, I'll bet, snipped at an angle, dipped in washes
of ultramarine, calligraphed the name
                                        Suleiman the Magnificent
we studied together on screen. Those letters—
crisp as pennons unfurling in their gallop
west across the vellum, just as the Ottoman vowed
he'd sweep, erasing infidels . . .
                            That is an impressive cursive! we all agreed.
The signature's curbed now under museum glass but unfaded,
undaunted, still flaunting
its old cojones in gold ink.

                    •   •   •

Straight to the water Chompsky trots, ignoring
my whistle and the baboons who nibble their seedpods
delicately as little crustless sandwiches
beneath the acacias
                        until, at the lake's edge, crab-pink ruffles shiver
and lift—a feather boa flung gabbling into the sky
as mutt meets mud with a smack—
                            flamingoes!

My chickadees, I breakfasted this morning on the sumptuous cake
of Sasol's *Birds of Southern Africa,* each species
tabbed in color on the text block like a fingerprint of jam. And now I greet
each bird in the bush by human name . . . *Masked Weaver, Lilac-*
breasted Roller, Red-eyed Bulbul, my hike become
an appellation trail . . .
                        Bulbul, Arabic for "nightingale"—a word
migrated down the flank of a continent as rich
in languages as minerals . . . flown south from Dar es Salaam
in some baffled slaver's brain? Who survived the harsh terrain

long enough to hang his syllables on this fistful of sub-Saharan
twitter, spectacular for its floral orbital ring
if not its song?

                  It's true, the birds here look like flowers. And the flowers
beak and claw themselves with thorn. Softness falls prey
unless it's prickly, peppery, or poisonous. Nasturtiums, gone feral
and sharp on the tongue since my friend Martin Masulay-
Masulay coaxed them to blossom from seed,
spread from old tomato cans he's set beside the trail. I sniff
their restive odor, like metal, licked . . .
                             Mornings, Martin unlocks
the gate, walks the park's perimeter checking for poachers
or squatters who come to cut acacia wood, then gives his plants a drink
from another can, humming a song whose words he says are dipped
not from the rivers of Oshiwambo or Lozi
he learned to paddle off at the regional school,
but from Subiya, his earliest rivulet.
                         The barbarian's luxury is to relish
new languages first as music. When Martin sings, I catch just one phrase
he's taught me,
                but chickadees, it must be our species' dearest cliché, to praise
mwezi when it rises, full and fertile, rinsed clean
at last in the rainy season.

                By now on a Sunday, Martin's been
and gone. The pool of shadow each acacia poured across the plain at sunup
drains back into its roots. The trail's a silver thread
stitched through the thirsting silver grasses.

                         Ahead, something buffs itself
across the chamois of the dust—

Martin's said don't worry: sure, there's snakes
everywhere you step, but only seven bite
so badly that, without the proper antidote,
you're toast. (Though understand, if nipped by even
the smallest smiling baby mamba, you'll want
just three things: shade, some paper, and a pencil. Get comfortable
and write your goodbye note. You'll only need
a single sheet of paper.)
                    Chompsky leashed and lunging, I try to read
the vanished scribbler's signature, faint *Ss* carving the sand
like waves. Or scales. Sinuous as those needle-fine dragon-scale waves
etching the surface of da Vinci's globe we googled
last week in class. Those lines that stunned us—cut by hand
before electricity!—on the glued-together fatter halves
of two blown eggs, laid by ostriches shipped live from Africa
north to the viscounts of Milan . . .
                    And the globe's Americas
still guesswork, vague shapes the maker seemed to think
hardly worth the trouble of visiting amid the writhing
waters scratched around them, *hic sunt*
dracones, and inked blue black with ash . . .
(You nailed it in your tween deadpan, Ndoshi: *Eish,*
Miss, who'd wanna land up there, eh?)

        •   •   •

                    What a curator
the mind is, restless, can't stop building these scrappy
cabinets of curiosities when walking for an hour. Or late on nights
not sleeping. Some veil blows off,
and I find myself childlike
among maps or birds or languages or
the origins of instruments,

                              out there with a boy in what's today
Afghanistan, guarding his brother's sheep
in the desert, only rocks to talk to. On the fortieth night, vexed or bereaved
or lovelorn, he moons beneath the cliché beauty until, seeing a scrap of catgut twin
lacing his pack, he winds it over a stick to pluck, then slowly tests its sound
when rubbed by cloth, leather, long hairs from his horse's tail—

                                                        I follow
that aggrieved and almost-living voice
as it evolves along a single string
into the rebaba Ibn Khaldun heard on his travels
and on into the rebec the Moors carried to Andalusia beside spices
and the names of stars, morphing through
invention's convivencias
into the violin,
                    whose chastened sob
even the most jaded listener centuries later
one snowy night alone in America
might hear and, hearing, be surprised
by tears beginning in her ears.

                        Why sounds so often
soften me, I don't know. Distant constant rivers
of traffic. Tree frogs' bells. Morning recess at the school across the road. Low
voices long ago on radios left murmuring in the barn
to soothe the fitful ponies . . .
                              And voices still
alive on tape. My parents, whose laughter
I can't remember, caught for a minute joking at some party
with my aunt. Lotte Lenya, Chet Baker, Sarah Vaughan . . . low breath, low note, slu
pulled through a wedding ring so slowly
it threatens to snag,

unraveling
until the listener's throat contracts . . .

There ought to be a cenotaph
to that boom box in the conservatory dorm, spooling a pale filament
back and forth between the reels, sweet companion giving every tremolo
a slightly underwater echo and only rarely
snarling some favorite's entrails
into a birds' nest of plastic
no mating songs would burble from again.
                                        The mix tapes
I made on that box . . . its fat satisfying buttons' click
for fast-forward and rewind
and stop, the pause
                when I was 23, 24

                —and chickadees, though I'll never speak of this,
when all the talents I'd sharpened to a point
snapped off, there were months
marked on no calendar
traced in no one's book
I fell in with a man, twice my age, whose signs
were hard for me to read except to know
he was magnetic, brilliant, sad, and a species
of married.
              Our nest: soft days caged in anonymous hotels. And nights—
how many—ten? a dozen? On the last, he licked his fingers clean of the cocaine
and his lips became a buzzing star. Each kiss made a little mouthful of my body
disappear, until my surface was a sky tongued full of open space the brilliant
dark burned through . . .

                Then came words: letters, scores of letters, buoyant

dopamine-fueled paper airplanes we flew above the turbulence
we caused. Devoutly we practiced the ancient rituals: stamps
and envelopes. Foolscap bitten by the teeth
of urgent type. Epic compilations taped
one for the other, their insert cards scrawled with notes
insisting the sender ravished by the other's
absent hearing . . .

                  What's most astonishing, in retrospect, are the hours
a composer—well-regarded, professional,
discreet—found to squander in epistles
with a girl.
          Waxing long
through June, long and slow and deep in salts
July wrung out of us on separate coasts, through August's
purple loosestrife blossoming, and goldenrod, and only
with the shortening daylight
did it wane.
          A fit of calenture.
                    By expensive overnight mail
came his final letter. (It needed only
a single sheet of paper.)

      •   •   •

Panting, up the switchback
at the lake's far edge Chompsky scrabbles,
past rock faces scoured by winds
breathing here between the Namib and the Kalahari
since long before mammals evolved
to sniff for distant rain,
                  sandstone veined with quartz
and flecked with other ores Martin calls

magnetic. If you spend much time out here, he says, you'll have
strange dreams, you'll hear strange music.

  • • •

           I've heard it.

  • • •

               I hear it now, filtered
through my idiosyncratic eardrums so it's partly wind on rock, part
Gottschalk, playing an instrument I can't help thinking of
as African
     since his pianos, or parts of them, were born, as the bulbul flies,
not far from here. If we could see
his Chickering, keys yellow where his fingers pressed their butters
into the veneer, we'd be seeing where his touch
signed its human feeling
with another's body, we'd be seeing the telltale line
finer than a hair snipped from a nursing elephant's head
where the wafers of ivory join.
The mark of the genuine.
       We'd taste
the names of trading posts like black pepper
cracked across our tongues: Ujiji, Bagamoyo, Zanzibar. In dreams
we'd catalogue the trek, each tusk that reached the coast
costing, through hunger and disease,
five native bearers' lives.
       At Zanzibar, tusks
taller than a man and wide as young elm trunks were packed so tightly
the holds seemed full of trees harvested from a forest
of ghosts.
    To Connecticut the tusks were shipped.
          There, in sleepy little Ivoryton,

my grandfather and kindly men like him spent decades tooling
delicate articles for toiletries and games. Broad-toothed combs
and slender toothpicks, letter openers
scalloped across the handles with miniature families
of elephants. Ladies' chinoiserie fans. Dice and billiard balls.
Piano keys. Ivoryton's piano keys for sixty years filled concert halls
and country parlors with the Chopin and Gottschalk and Bach
my aunt's playing taught me to love.
                                        I know that telltale line
by touch, the keys
on her old petite grand warming, my fingers
moving too small, too clumsily at first, then faster, with her tutoring
more skillful and at home
until, by the time I'd reached your age, chickadees, she'd smiled at me and said
now the piano was truly mine.
                                        It must have been the summer after that
I started learning Gottschalk's *Bamboula,* thrilling in
the power I felt arise from nothing
but my focus and my breath, my left hand's louring delay
before attack, as if an August breeze were gathering veils of cloud
implacably into thunderheads
within my body, becoming the storm I summoned
each day after school as the river carried hours past the window
and I loosed myself from all the hooks
of home.
                That piece got me into the conservatory. Into
my composer's orbit. Once in a while even now I'll finger a bit of it
along my desk's edge as I'm sitting and waiting, you with quills in hands
bent over a quiz. Though it was so long ago. So long ago and someone else
practicing, someone altogether else assuredly, then less assuredly
playing those recitals it must have been clear to all who heard them
were diligent performances by a pupil whose gifts, fine

as they were, would never overflow
the banks of her tributary talent.

                            It's so long ago I can listen to the Gottschalk again
without envy, with pleasure, even . . . though to hear it played well, *really* well,
still hollows me a little. He wrote it in France at 24, the same age
I was on leaving the conservatory. He was delirious
with typhoid, the story goes; he was remembering
music carried from what today is Gambia and Senegal
to his childhood New Orleans. What we hear
below its notes is Gottschalk's overhearing
an echo of migrations, a dance
maybe evolved from a cradle song maybe
evolved from a song for walking
long distances
far from home
through different languages.

        •   •   •

A continent as rich in languages as minerals . . .

                                 where even a human
can learn to read the Honeyguide
who's learned to read humans, leading them
burring and whistling to hives his bill alone
can't burgle . . .

                Chompsky aside, the animals I've followed
intimately are dead. Gone, the long marled skein
of Dinah's purr, and Suzy whickering
winter mornings in the barn.
                       And what a hooved
gut-kick in Damascus each time I saw a row of camels' heads
hewn off and hung outside a butcher shop, tongues

slung out, blood gleaming at their throats
to advertise *Fresh Meat.* The souk
electric, jostling, full of noise
fell silent in those felted ears, the impossible
eyelashes grown to block blown sand
become stiff ladders
for flies

        —a decade back! Time holds its breath,
chickadees, because you aren't any older than
my students there at the American School . . .

                        Only Chompsky
has aged, distinguished fellow whiskered now
like my grandfather in white . . .

                    No snakes
or acacias there. No flamingoes. Never did I hear
the legendary bulbul. But the old city itself
absorbed me. On summer afternoons the women's
washroom behind the Umayyad Mosque whiffed
of sweaty hair, let down for a few minutes while its owners
slipped off hijab and palmed cool water up to the unwrapped
backs of necks and throats. A sympathy of odors, and a wedge
of space offered to the stranger among the bodies
bending at the sink; she's merely one
among a multitude, rinsing
her sticky face. I'd nose the souk, a labyrinth
complex as my solitude, through which I'd orient
my steps by following the smell of cardamom
past coffee stalls, until its greenish sharpness braided into
wet slate and algae bloom. An ancient fountain
stood on a corner, pink plastic cup chained to its spout
so all might drink. (It moved me so, that cup; people would stop

and pass it hand to hand, giving their children sips.)
                                                    I'd pick up
the alkali tang of hot basalt, trailing it from shade into a sunlit square,
and there, whatever distances I'd carried within me dissolved
among Sunnis and Shias eating shish kebab, Maronites and Alawites
licking ice creams stiff with mastic, Circassians and Nestorians and Kurds
and old Druze men and quiet Jews scraping peppery smears of muhammara
off their plates with rags of bread. Bedouins and Palestinians looked alike to me
until I learned to read their semaphore of scarves.
                                                    Lemon, sumac, and smoke
from grilling lamb would lead me past them all toward the little city gate
where, long ago, Tamerlane piled the heads of Damascenes. There
in the butchers' street I was the barbarian, loving the luxury of being
the shortest footnote in
someone else's epic.
                        For weeks, that was plenty.

But one day in an antique land, a traveler longs to drop
her flâneurie's hauteur. She sees a camel's head
bleeding in a butcher's door. Bracing herself
on a breath, she enters, marshals book-learned verbs
and fuck-all nerve, tries a phrase, repeats, adds
pantomiming hands and—*Mash'Allah!*—exchanges
coins for a kilo of camel loin.
                        And then . . .
                                    —what djinn
shoved me? Pleasure in speaking, being spoken to
and understood, remembering the word for *head*
sent such an adrenalin rush to mine
I asked to buy the one at the door.
                        Quickly the butcher
flensed cheek flaps loose, scooped from its sockets

the frozen stare, sawed free the foot of tongue.
He wrapped the skull in cling film. Oozing, it shone
lucent dark jellies. From septum to poll, it stretched
longer than my torso. It must have weighed ten kilos. Cradling it
like an awkward baby, I carried it from the shop.

Unctuous, all afternoon the loin braised. That night, it melted
my guests. Even the shy Goethe Institute librarian
took seconds. Forking another mouthful, her Norwegian lover
pronounced it *more flavorful than minke whale,* and my favorite colleague
—still tipsy, he said, after a two-day rave
where he'd *blown a mullah's nephew to kingdom come*
in an old crusader castle—tongued the dish to soft-core pun
with camels oiling the eyes of needles and needing
rich men's needling, till he'd broken laughter's back
with straws of horn.
                        Next day, hung under,
I put the skull in a kettle of water bubbling with salt
and Dettol. It steamed the kitchen with its fetor, mutton darkness
stewed with wet Band-Aid. All afternoon
it ticked against the pot. Slowly the bones sighed out
their slicks of brownish grease.
                        That's all your brain is, too, I thought.
A froth. Some flot, some jet. Memory. It made me
queasy, then quiet.
                        When the bones were clean, I hung the skull outside
so air and sun could dry it. For weeks I left it. At night, wind mouthed
its surface like a woodwind's reed, loosing weird thin notes from it
as if the far-off desert stars made sound.

    • • •

As if, chickadees, Orion
stalked over me
carrying no club, no sword, but a flute
carved from mammoth bone. Or an instrument more Levantine
and a little wheezy . . . a mijwiz, maybe, subduing Taurus
by wootling until the dizzy constellations spin around them
in a dabke, and the Dog Star I think of as Laika's ghost
nips wildly at their heels . . .

                    How strange, now, being so far
south . . . looking up at night I sometimes feel the flashing
shiv of *wherewherewhere?* Orion's no frozen hunter
climbing the winter midnight's stairs. No hunter
at all—you've got a circus acrobat, heels
over head, cartwheeling across
the summer sky, his belt
                Alnitak Alnilam Mintaka
                              skewed,
jeweled scabbard flipped up
into a heart.
        Upside down!
        I think every night as he rises,
        and it takes me a second to catch myself
        reminding myself
        the stars are not what's changed

   •   •   •

or changing.

      Flamingoes fringe the lake again
as we pick our way down toward the car. Baboons doze, shaded . . . five,

six, eight, postprandial, barely deigning
to glance up as I unlock the door.
                              They're so smart. I could learn
a thing or two from them . . .
                              It's good to get in and sit
motionless, shaded in the driver's seat, windows
down. Going nowhere for a bit. Chompsky parks
his head on my knee.
                    He snores.
                         A laughing dove
nesting above us in the acacia bubbles
the fountain in her throat. Going nowhere
                              I press play,

fingering the wheel's rim
as the mature Glenn Gould hands me
through a veil of wear on the old CD the golden-fleshed
Bosc pears of Bach, each bite of the Goldbergs
releasing a little gush of nectar
into my blood stream.

                    His fingers
traveling through these notes
can assuage, I think,
all pain.

            Last year, I must have listened to them
every day. The alarm would jab its knitting needle
into my ear, I'd hit the snooze, and I'd have roused
for nothing had I lacked the tiny crumbs
of hunger gathering around the word
bagels. Lucky body, it never lost its appetite, even as

some cravings—or half-cravings, really; inconstant,
absent at times, at times desperate as the longing
for salt—went unfed, and the Christmas rains washed away
my forty-fourth year, and it was clear, finally,
in the end my body would belong
only to me.
                    Centuries of migrants, their signatures
Xed inside the cells passed down to me
by those two travelers
whose hands I'd held so briefly, had reached
their final port.

                    The armature of habits
my days had built themselves around
bent under me. I'd exhausted
all the stars and needed the erasure
of sleep. Chompsky would stretch himself
beside me, bulb of his nose
screwed into my armpit's socket, or with his limpid
seal's face breathing on my cheek, and I'd inhale
his valor with its mildly catfish odor.
                              I'd try not thinking
of all I'd never learn . . . birthday cakes shaped
like mermaids / robots / frogs / firetrucks—never
to burn my thumbs pulling them
from the oven. Never to lose my temper
wrestling pairs of footy pajamas into a silly
rolling turtle suitcase. No fingernails so tiny I'd fear
scissors and bend to nip their soft wax
with my teeth . . . What knowledge would feed
the coming years, if none of this?

                                    I'd known
a loved body beside me in the bed, swallows
skirling through the dusk outside, and voices
in a language so familiar I might have dreamt it
passing below our window while light
flickered like a fountain's endlessly wrecked
and remade surface across the ceiling. And a street
where men on winter mornings steamed their faces
over bowls of breakfast fuul. My fingers knew the horsetail
scritch of a lion's mane, rough hanks shorn close
so the radio collar keeping him safe from poachers
fit least troublingly against his purr. Tranquilized,
he slept. I brought the handful of mane
up to my face. It smelled
                         —like what?
It wasn't rank. If anything, it smelled grassy, clean
as a dog's head after he rolls in an August field
tall with loosestrife and goldenrod. But it wasn't even that,
exactly. It had no referent. I soothe myself
sometimes by trying to puzzle out
words for the essence of lion before I sleep.

In those extinguished weeks I'd take long walks.
Even now, once in a while, something overheard
nudges loose a sound learned earlier in
another place, some sign shorn of sense
and context, some gently floating
comb jelly of language, *vetro soffiato*
or *tawus* or *the rainy Hyades* brushing their clear
tickling vowels along my synapses
so gently and so deeply they flush me

with their beauty. I find myself
in tears. Is it hormonal? I can't say if it's a peculiar
hot flash, or adaptive primate response
to prickling in my Broca's region, or a species
of fruitless love.
                         Because love starts in the head,
I know. It's small still, but its soft kicks
move me the longer I'm here listening
to you, chickadees.
                         Or it can start *with* a head . . .
an aria da capo. Wasn't love the seed messily
implanting itself that day in Damascus
I elbow-flagged a taxi, my hands cradling
a swaddled bébé of camel skull? And not just
any taxi, chickadees: a car whose driver, muffled
in his keffiyeh, squinted gravely through
ropes of prayer beads, his rearview mirror
more mosque's screen than reflecting pool,
to gauge what non-native potentially invasive
specimen I was. His radio thickened the air between us
with the noontime recitation of Koran. But he was
formal, courtly, and would not discard
the prescribed courtesies with which the Muslim
greets the stranger. Welcome. Was I well? My simple answers
seemed to satisfy. He paused, easing the taxi
like a needle into the rushing traffic's vein. Did I like
the city? Sir, your city is sweet. He beamed. And how many
children had I? Hearing the half-wry reply
I'd evolved for exactly these occasions, his eyes
lifted in the mirror and—I'm sure I read him rightly—
moistened as he paled, promising me he'd pray

until, with Allah's blessing, I conceived one. And maybe
years later, having survived the war, he's praying
still? He went on, his words
weaving through suras their soft benedictions
while about the dragon's head I held
politely asked no questions.

FADO

Words are for those with promises to keep.
—W. H. AUDEN

Dogs' feelings aren't complex, you say; they lack
our nuances of mood. They look
sad when we leave them, sure, and their joy at a roll
in deer poo's indisputable. But they don't mull
over what they've done
badly. No guilt bites them. No pre-dawn
sorrow yawns . . .

               Well, maybe you're right—
but then, what's gnawing at my pup? Each night
he howls, accompanied by wheezes
from a squeaky chicken toy he squeezes
balefully with his front paw.
He cries as if all faith is flawed.
I've laughed at my companion
pumping his slapstick *bandoneon,*
then sobered at the ache his notes reveal.
Some sorrow at the heart of things
haunts the rubber chicken's songs
and he responds until, lonesome as a train's whistle
late in the darkness, his wails unsettle
a valve my throat
must struggle to keep shut.
The chicken has no minor chords.
The dog's expressiveness wants words.
Still, that strain descends
into the human soul and sounds
depths only the inarticulate can feel.

SENTIMENTAL EDUCATION

The new hormones built me a sense of smell
3-D, architectural.

I could measure rooms' volumes
by the density of perfumes
curdling in the air.

From down the hall behind three doors
tight shut, whiffs of my lover's shampoo
queased back to the bedroom, florid pink jellies
slicking down to sugar
the biscuit of his nape.

Cheese scraps pared and scraped into the sink
baited complex traps of stink
set to spring in the apartment's heat.

Strange metamorphic creature—
half mutt nose / half mouse terror
at whom the least reek
bared its teeth.

A lick of margarine
barked and bit, metallic.

Even bread wasn't innocent.
Its yeasts were simply waiting till I started sniffing
to ferment.

I'm a dog, I thought.

But some part of me couldn't stop tugging
as far as my sense's leash would allow

and it was almost worth the nausea's swallow
to leave my body there
below the sheet, and follow a draft out through the screen—

past the porch, the yard, the rot-spiced knot-pine fence
hunched over its hibiscus crutch; past the live oaks'

mushroom-musky nets of moss; beyond
the on-ramp to the overpass, the freeway's scorched

oils and vinyls, chlorides and smokes, and the airport's kerosene; out
further than the shrimp boats rocking toylike on the swells

to where the salt skirts of a rainstorm
just beginning to gather in loose bellying folds above the gulf
dragged their hem in the sea and grew
damp with a clean ozone ruffle.

I asked to stay awake through the procedure.

And for a week or so after
as the hormones faded
was visited by ghostly odors.

Water drying.

The iron in stones.

SOME SAY

after Sappho, fragment 16

When I look at him and feel under my ribs
a Sukhoi T-50 performing a Pugachev's Cobra
    no longer as an evasive maneuver
but for the thrilling thrust-vector stomach plunge,
    and my limbic system's an alembic
distilling chilled champagne from rocket fuel,
    and my gray hairs are the smoke off ships
whose burning all night bloodied the eastern sky
    before dawn doused their charcoal spars
in cold light, whitening his beard with ash,
    and in the flotsam washed to the beach
we find a ring, a feather, a key, a watch,
        then twenty years collapse like a star;
        we're children, giggling again at the altar.

            •   •   •

The night I knew   *That one*

    Hackles up I snapped at his throat hot bark I
    could not swallow unkenneled self
    gone feral my words all canine and carnassial

    And him raising against me finally
    one eyebrow turning away on his pillow leaving
    me licking my salt and singular fury

    Cheek pressed to drain below the pissing
    shower for hours I lay gutted by the cool
    blade of his refusal even to enter the fray

    That one.   All night an army of ships
    of horses an army of men on foot marched
    through me   And him   unarmed   unharmed

on the black earth   sleeping

WESTERN WIND

Thunder woke us.

Then we lay
awake in darkness,
listening to the rain.

Neither spoke.

Wind ticked
freshened leaves
against the screen.

Our silence held
no distance

but the distance
coming months
would bring.

Neither spoke.

For absence, no solace
but presence.

Awake together
in the darkness.

A little longer in
the same bed,
the same weather.

ELEGY FOR ESTROGEN

Without which the tits, anxious
    rabbits, sit up no longer on their haunches
in the sun nibbling grasses,
    but cower, fine fat alertnesses
pressed flat, who sense
    the raptor's presence.
And the chin, ample in
    its sympathy, sinks down,
laying the folded
    pleats of its old
coat upon the lawn to lap the dew.
    Must the cunt, too,
lament this loss?
    Atrophies dwindle once-
trophied glades, whose rivulets
    rinsed the helmets
of kings? What balm, after lush
    spring and summer's flush
fall dumb,
    to say wisdom will come
pressing its cool cabbage leaf across my brow?

    Let all perfumes perish now.

This insistence
    clocks can be stopped with resistance
insults. The one relief
    at a certain age
is at last being sage
    enough to admit when I feel bereft.
I've little time left
    for lies
meant to anesthetize
    grief.

WISHES FOR FIFTY

Face worn well, though
well-worn. Not timorous,
no shrinking. A pup's nose
still for the raw and stinky.
Deep pleasure gnawing
your bone of work. Neither
so sapless you can't weep,
nor barked in oak like those
Can't-Be-Wrongs. New songs.
Martini glass astringed
with a drop of dry
skepticism before the gin;
nonetheless, your verre
ever half-full, and trust
enough in the future
to plant asparagus.
It's obvious you'll never
step in that river again.
But let your mind spill
now and then with sources
you'd skinny-dip
once more if you could.
Intimacies? Let there be
lascivity with sexy
librocubicularists. Loneliness
only in tonic doses
for its delicious silences.
And dusks, when memory's
a glass jar dipped from a stream
with curls of murk
wildly turning: let them settle
until the water clears.

So clear it tempts
your sip. *Salud*—
here's water under
all the bridges
you burned.

CLICHÉ

Its back and forth, ad nauseum,
ought to make the sea a bore. But walks along the shore

cure me. Salt wind's the best solution for
dissolving my ennui in,

along with these protean
sadnesses that sometimes swim

invisibly
as comb-jelly

a glass or two of wine below my surface.
Some regrets

won't untangle. Others loosen as I watch the waves
spreading their torn nets

of foam along the sand
to dry. I walk and walk and walk and walk, letting their haul

absorb me. One seal's hull
scuttled to bone staves

gulls scream
wheeling above. And here . . . small, diabolical,

a skate's egg case,
its horned purse nested on pods of bladder-wort

that still squirt
brine by the eyeful. Some oily slabs of whale skin, or

—no, just an
edge of tire

flensed from a commoner leviathan.
Everywhere, plastic nurdles gleam

like pearls or caviar
for the avian gourmand

and bits of sponge dab the wounded wrack-line,
dried to froths of air

smelling of iodine.
Hours blow off down the beach like spindrift,

leaving me with an immense
less-solipsistic sense

of ruin, and, as if
it's a gift, assurance

of ruin's recurrence.

OF VINEGAR OF PEARL

The elements return to the body of their mother.
—PARACELSUS

1.

Like pulp-and-spittle wasps' nests
built in their season to last
only until winter, bones
crumble in her as she sits.
She sections the day's clemen-
cies into mouthfuls, hawks out
any bitter pips, swallows
good pungence with sips of smoke
—Lapsang Souchong or Laphroaig,
depending on the hour—
preferring solitude to
solicitude from the kind,
including her children who
were hard to bear and are hard
now to hear. Nine decades have
drawn her, masterwork of ten-
don and vein illustrating
frailty condensing to one
ferocious node, a will still
refusing to cede. But now?
When the heart no longer turns
the blood's tide. When fluid pools,
refusing to be sluiced back
into its channels. She's walked
so far down the strand that seals
barely lift their heads as she
steps over them, returning
finally to her sisters.

She's up to her knees now in
a flosh of her body's own
sea-wash. Dying? Or dying-
ish? Is this it? Is it this?

2.

Her limbs are Lear's daughters
—all promise, then paring away
the tyrant's power with refusals
small at first, then cruel.
On clement afternoons we drive
out to a paved greenway
curving along the esker where,
as her doctor advised, she plows
to and fro behind her walker
following an invisible mule.

There's no help I can give
but silence, trailing her dogged
rows. Then their reversals.
It's on the third carve slowly up
the furrow her body's cut
before me I begin to think
if I were a landscape feature
I would be an esker, my distinctive
sediments layered below
a once-imposing glacier
now going extinct.

3.

You're the meanest bitch I've ever known
I hiss. It's venomous; a curse
below the breath is somehow worse.
(Does she have her hearing aids turned on?)

Well you're a dictator! You micromanage everything!
she howls back, livid. (Yes.) I've organized
doctors, insurance, prescriptions, bed.
Neither diagnosis is wrong.

We dose each other with silence.
At suppertime, she comes downstairs to test
her patience once more with my presence.
Wine palliates. We limp through the visit.

• • •

Outside her room's door each morning
I stall, steeling myself
—is she still herself?
Or stolen off?—
until I can face anything.

Slowly, I open. Every morning it surprises me
how soothed I am by her expression
buttoning its scorn back on
as she eyes my tray's offering
of toast and jam and tea.

4.

They say the mother's death is hardest. Her body
our first loss, burying or burning it repeats
the fleshy severance we can't remember, though
our limbic systems bear the ultraviolet tattoo
of birth, when adrenaline rushed through
our infant blood in floods no after-stress
surpasses. In death's black light,
those ink pricks glare.

                    Is this shock
the long-suspended echo of her emptiness
when her labor ended and I lay there, the anchoring
cord was cut, and I breathed the air?

            •   •   •

Alone, guest in a western town so spare the train
rattling through it cut each night in half, my mind
all day would void itself, and darkness
conjured ghosts of long-forgotten talk. Late,
a whistle pulled me drowning from the lake
of sleep, and there I found myself in a summer
decades back. Decades back, my mother had phoned
unable to catch her breath. She was calling from her station,
from the platform payphone, and I could hear
watery rushing behind her, like surf or rainy traffic.
Her train had come and she'd boarded first, she said,
to get a forward seat. As she'd settled in, a man,
delayed somehow, somehow running from
the parking lot across the tracks, had ducked
beneath the guardrail. She'd heard a shout
as her window shuddered with a flashing
thunder, an express blown through along

the other line, not stopping. She'd seen
the man caught in the narrow scrim
between the trains, she'd caught his eyes
and held them there an arm's-length off
beyond the glass, held his eyes with hers,
the piston of her pulses in her ears
how many beats
till something snagged
and pulled him under.

She'd had to tell someone
about his eyes. Though she could barely press
her words through the payphone's static
and what I realized then
was chaos at the station, though
months had passed since we'd last spoken,
it was me she telephoned, I was the one
to whom she gave that look.

•　•　•

Walking the rails through the desert to clear my head, I reached a sort of shelter
    no taller than my shoulder, where a trestle crossing a gully

nested a clutter of tumbleweeds. Bones of antelope and cactus lay around,
    and plastic flowers from the little graveyard there, dumped,

I guessed, when their color leached and they resembled too much what lay
    beneath the stones. Animal, vegetable, mineral—haven't I

always been a stone? Restless wind curried the grasses. It was still
    too cold for rattlesnakes, so I crouched and sat on the rocks

below the sleepers reeking of creosote. From the telephone wires along the tracks
    the wind wrung various pitches, as if testing

how loudly it must speak to reach a distant listener. Over and over it made connection
    and broke it off. Then, growing out of the wind, I heard

a second voice, distinct though far away. And the idea came as if spoken: *Lie down.*
    Below the trestle I stretched along the rocks. The sky

between the sleepers was very clean, very blue, very uninvolved. The wind in the wire
    spoke a long time above the train until, keening,

the voices merged. Thunder mourned over me. I lay open-eyed to feel
    how close could I get to that voice without that voice crushing me.

5.

Secretly the animals of my childhood gave birth in nests, in dens, in holes, in darkness, but our pig farrowed out in her penyard one windy afternoon in March. Fourteen piglets. Exhausted, she rolled over on the runt. With a broom I jumped into the yard to swat her off the screaming stub. Up she lunged, enraged, enormous, brute instinct fleshed, four times my body-weight, smashing me to the fence. My mother reached over the gate, got me below the arms, yanked. A crush, a heave and a crash, a whiplash flail as she hauled me out. My skull flung back, cracking her face. Pig shrieks, after-birth, my mother's blood gouting from her nose I'd knocked aslant. Later that summer I "became a woman" as the dainty manual for ladies left on the bookshelves by some great aunt during the Coolidge administration put it. A pallid stain and rending pain. My mother gave me whisky poured slowly over a sugar cube.

6.

Thou art thy mother's glass   thou art

and she
she in thee
          O she in thee

calls back   (how soon)

calls back the lonely April of her prime

      •   •   •

Truly, we learn how things hold together only by watching
            things break down. Carbon-14 decays
      measurably into its daughter elements; through them,
        we leap backward in time to the wet spring
            this bone chip went browsing among

fern glades in the rib of a doe. She lipped at budtips, her sides
            fat with fawn. Today in the gully's
      bottom, rusted baling wire and the silt of windshields
        crushed fine return their borrowed minerals
            to the dirt. Cola-bottle tears

mirror my glances. But what good are mirrors? Or tears? Their salt
            gnaws through the ages. As tears decayed
      the Restoration's tooth for ragged grief. Audiences
        craved their *King Lear* sweet as a girl's whisky
            spooned over sugar; Cordelia

lived to kiss the salt from her father's eyes and balm her too-true
            words with words of love. *And what are tears*
      but mirrors? I found penciled in my mother's high school *Lear.*

Now I reflect on her. In my pocket
        compact dabbing on lipstick, it's

her sneer I gloss. And when my other pocket rips its ragged
        velvet lining out each month, I fear
    what mirror it might come to hold. And she who'd pulled me from
      her own pocket, like a magician stunned
        to find a small pink rabbit there—

I must have always sensed how near she always was to breaking,
        for when she broke I was scared but not,
    it struck me as I watched her weep, surprised. When the body
      of love decays, we see the skeleton
        beneath. We sat in her parked car

after she'd lost her home. She cried furiously, wordlessly,
        saying only that she wanted me
    to let her go. Go? Where? Where at eighty, homeless, savings
      spent, boxes of books jammed in the trunk and
        two blind and incontinent dogs

panting in the back seat, does one *go*? She had a tent, she screamed,
        she'd camp, just let her be. If asking
    my mother how she'd gotten here felt like slashing a blade
      of broken mirror across her face, then
        stopping her when she tried to leave

flayed love to the bone. *She couldn't hear my gentle words, yet she/*
        surrendered to my strength. Stronger than
    she looked. Flailing. Before she collapsed in my hold that was
      stranger than a hug. I snipped my panic
        into bearable syllables.

That's how we broke it down together. Disarticulation.
We've never spoken about it since.
Slowly, with no visible scission, her glib surfaces
returned. *(And art thou not thy mother's glass?)*
She came into my house; we ate

sandwiches; gladly her dogs relieved themselves, then slept. Later,
ignoring her protests, we helped her
find a nearby rental. Sometimes I'll see her in a store
or at the post office, and if she re-
cognizes me, she'll say hello.

7.

Mother of vinegar   Mother of pearl

And of the elements: "These four figures be called the *mothers*, whereof the first is attributed to the fires, the second to the air, the third to waters, the fourth to the earth."

And in the earth is found the filtrous substance named by miners "mother coal."

And in the body's hidden mines, by "mother" they mean the womb whose traveling brings madness.

Or madness itself. Thus Lear, unhoused and at his daughters' mercy: "O how this mother swels up toward my heart!"

And therefore remedies. "For the Accident of the Mother, they doe burn Feathers, and by these Ill-smells the Rising of the Mother is put down."

Or the child put down. From Mayhew's *London Labour and the London Poor*: "My husband can't do nothink but give the babies a dose of 'Mother's Blessing' (that's laudanum, Sir, or some sich stuff) to sleep 'em when they're squally."

And through the base of laudanum to "mother's ruin," slang for gin.

Mother of the cocktail, whose first instance Pliny recounts as Cleopatra, drawing from her ear the finest pearl the world had ever known, dropping it into a chalice of vinegar and then, when the gem dissolved, drinking it,

O Mother of vinegar   Mother of pearl

its minerals neutralizing the acid so the liquid was potable and bland.

8.

Lowered skies the morning I take her in,
then drizzling while we silently sign the forms
saying I'll be her voice if she can't speak.
Gowned and gurnied in Pre-Op, she brushes off my kiss
and I only know she's anxious when she asks
once, then a moment later asks me again
to water her garden, though now it's pouring.

•   •   •

astilbe   aster   aster   yarrow
height commanded by sunlight
low half in shadow   wild at the edges
wild carrot lips over lamb's ear
bee balm   butter-and-eggs beside tarragon
upstart crowsfoot and sunflower
volunteer by the feeder

here she scoffs at plants
fussed into lines like little sonnets
the impatiens marking her neighbor's yard
wanly off from the street *just making a place*
for dogs to piss

here boneset   beggarweed
beggarweed   vetch
little clitoral sweetpeas shy beneath unruly green
her sage a scented bravado
wagging its velvet sleeves well as any coxcomb

badged outcrops of roses gone feral
rough shrub for the mockingbirds' bed
beehive   wasps' nest

loam smell where she buried raw
a fox's skull beneath the white hydrangeas

• • •

Later she refuses the advised procedure to school her heart that's balking at its trot.

No I'll feel best if I have a cup of tea in my own bed and finish my book without more
   fuss.

(She's commandeered my Lady Mary Wortley Montague *Turkish Embassy Letters*,
   volume two.)

Her accomplice signs her out of the ward   yes   acknowledges the likelihood of   yes
has been advised that   yes   understands   yes yes   the grave   yes   risks without

• • •

Doctor, this is a woman who once buried a piano.
                                                Yes, had workmen
backhoe a trench by her garden, then trolley the upright
up to the edge and topple it in.
                          And then phoned me, pleased to be rid
at last of the junked-up box no one could play.

                  About the oddity of burying
                  a large musical instrument
                  she was utterly blasé.

                       And blasé when not long ago she said
I hid a razor in my shoe
                  We were eating birthday tiramisù at a place we'd picked
                  thinking she'd like the osso buco, and when I came
                  back from the mignon powder room I found

                                                thin chat had spun
                                                somehow to this
                                                unfurling this *I never*

told you? I thought I'd told you   while calmly
                                        spooning cream. She was so calm it seemed
                                        we must not dimple her surface
                                        with concern.

The '40s   you know   *it's what doctors did when they didn't know*
what else to do

                                        Electrodes, she remembered,
                                        and mild metallic
                                        headaches after, back in her locked room.

                                        Her roommate went on alternate days.

I saw from other women in the ward what I'd be like if I stayed
so I hid a razor

and would have used it

then my case came for review
I lied when asked if I felt better

                                        Calm, calm, running her spoon precisely along the cryst
                                        beveled edge

so they sent me home

            •   •   •

That night I dream a backhoe's blade
    chattermarking granite
until it finds the softer soil
    I hear workers lost in rain hear
buckets of sodden gravel
    tipping in the stones' rattle
the awful chuckle the wood struck
    wires' jangle the echoes'
falling before a quiet no
    years of burying will muffle

• • •

A memory: her in my childhood. It must be the early '70s. Something
wakes her, something's wrong. What is it? Downstairs all's fine, fine in the
kitchen, fine in the yard. She takes the flashlight and goes to the barn.
Breathing that should be there is not. No red eye glows from the stall. The
hinges' screws are stripped and the door leans aslant. Out to the shed, then,
where she's meant to fix the gate. Before he turns to her in the flashlight's
beam, she hears him. Hock-deep in sweetfeed from the fifty pound bag he's
gnawed open, he regards her steadily, jaws grinding. It's the most comforting
sound in the world, unless it's 4 a.m. and it's a horse who's gorged enough to
founder. A horse will eat himself to death. From the spill she tries to gauge
how much is gone. He's knocked the bag over and nosed the grain into a
mound like a pillow to which he dips his head. A honeyed pillow from gold-
en fields where she might close her eyes and dream… But you have to walk
a gorged horse to move the grain. She clips on the lead. Up and back, su e giù,
forth and return across the lawn. Ahead of the birds. Ahead of the roosters.
He isn't showing any pain, but he's jumpy and his chest feels hot to her hand.
To stay awake, she counts. Two hundred twelve steps with the right foot from
barn to road. Then back, counting the left—same number? A car passes;
someone already off to work. There, now isn't that where the white goose
appeared, at the edge of the road just there, blown one August by a hurri-

cane? Its wing was broken and they took it in and gave it brandy in an eye-dropper; it lived in an apple crate under the kitchen table. She was old enough then to read, and knew the tale where a goose speaks to a girl. *Alas, young queen, passing by.* They make another sweep of the yard. *Alas young queen,* was that Anderson? Grimm? No, wasn't it a horse that spoke? *If this your mother knew/ Her heart would surely break in two.* Falada was the horse's name, she remembers. Yes. It was her mother's horse that spoke to her. Her mother had sent her on a journey with Falada to keep her safe. But soon she had lost the handkerchief stained with her mother's royal blood that gave her power. Falada was killed. Now the townspeople thought she was only a poor girl who watched the geese. But the goosegirl hung the dead horse's head above the gate so she could hear it speak. *If this your mother knew,* it cried to her every morning. She had lost her bloodline and her mother. She had no friend in the world save dead Falada. Slowly the east pales to a watered green. *Alas young queen.* Then, in the space of a minute, the sky between the maples brightens and the morning star is doused. They walk till the horse's eye is cool dark liquid giving back a human form.

• • •

(is that why she's always liked books + animals + plants so v. much more than people?)

over the page your eyes
canter left to right
veer then ride the line
below until you're wide
awake yet hypnotized

had you fallen through
the solid part of *you*
into the cellar room

your self is built upon
—a room electrified
inside by puzzled men

until your eyes are lamps
lit by a stranger's hand
casting a shocked light
before their beams go dim—

free from that room again
wouldn't you crave the calm
eyes cantering alone
smoothly along the lines
the letters clear and crisp
moons pressed into the snow
white rows between the dark
hoofmarks you leave behind?

9.

But she also gave me confidence, for what's confidence but learning to slip
    your fingers in the hive's mouth to feel bees climbing up the ladders of
    your wrists?

To surrender to electric, ticklish bliss, unafraid of stings?

What's confidence but skinning a hung and gutted rabbit by pulling down its
    pelt, hocks to nose, the way you'd peel a sweater over your own head?

At oxers of sticks and milkcrates, being coaxed to ride till your shetland's
    cocked ears lead her over or she knocks the bars askew is a hell-bent,
    sometimes-useful confidence.

And when you're old enough to measure doses and tall enough to reach, it's
    being taught to free a foundered horse from pain by sliding tablets of
    phenylbutazone so deep behind his muscled tongue he can't spit them
    out again.

I've helped pour a pony-keg of beer into the trough for our favorite pig.

He sniffed the foam then swigged, swigged and swooned, then staggered up
    the ramp onto the butcher's truck, practically whistling.

> Child: (snuffling)
> Mother: *No tears no bacon.*

Armed with a knife below the mares'-tails of March, I've been taught to
    wound a branch precisely with a notch, fit a scion in the vee and tape the
    new limb tight so that in time, different kinds of apples will grow on a
    single tree.

10.

If we were people possessing depths
less opaque to ourselves,
we might reach our hands
down into the bitter
cold that gnaws the wrist
bones, down toward the bottom
and scoop the ticklish
starfish, the spiked urchin,
the muscled unsettling
sea cucumber of feeling
up into words and lay them
between us on the rocks
from which, it is clear, soon
she must swim out
while I must watch.

      •   •   •

Into the clasp of the oyster's
     purse I slip the knife's
edge, nudging the wedge
     with steady pressure. Patience
meets resistance. I rock the blade
     along the fissure, applying
torque. A towel blocks
     my palm from cuts, silting
up with flecks of mud
     and chips of shell, this
resilience's refusal to undo
     its locks until, with a reluctant
suck and slide, metal
     breaches the valve and the halves
divide. One wrist-twist

unties the muscle. The oyster
glisters like memory
        in its cradle. Not tipping
its liquors, I pass my mother
        the living sip. She turns
her fist over, opening
        her hand into a cup. (Braced
on her cane, her hip's pain
        mellowed by wine and
a little more wine, she's
        leaning at the sink to watch
me shuck.) I wince
        lemon over the tang.
Slowly she bends to its juice
        and slurps—*Delicious!*
So you have one useful skill!
        Waves across a shoal, one
for me another for her
        I open and we eat the dozen
standing there, survivors
        of another week, filling
the sink with empty shells
        till it looks like a wreck's flank
scabbed with nacre barnacles.

II.
The truth?
I love her as fresh meat loves salt.

Rivers weeping through shallows
below an abyss of wheeling stars—

what stinging elements
go, unmarked, to make us?

This is my salary:
one tear,
brine enough for savor.

And my inheritance:

dandelions, *dent-de-lyon*, little fanged
hungers strewing the garden
among the lilies

      —from them
when I was young my mother braided me
      a crown of lion's teeth.

(R. P. 1924–2021)

EUPHORBIA

Euphorbia damarana, endemic to Namibia

Not euphoria. This shrub
oozes a latex so toxic
    eleven miners living
out near Uis went off fossicking

    wood to cook their pap en vleis
and, kindling fire with its twigs,
    inhaled its smoke . . . then woke up
dead before breakfast (or so goes

    the bush myth). But if you're a
San hunter needing to poison
    your arrowheads for duiker,
or American amateur

    gardener planting borders
of spurge in some city locus
    amoenus or provincial
eden, members of the genus

    Euphorbia grow welcome
as rain in the Kalahari.
    They're familiar to me, since
as things have evolved, my children

    are all vegetable. I choose
annuals and perennials
    based on their hardiness in
zones deranged by climate changes

or new to me as I range
far from home. With mixtures of de-
    caying fish and decocted
ordure of horses, with tinctures

    dosed out in grains to obtain
just the nitrogen-phosphorous
    concord rotting affords and
fertility craves, I coax them

    to bloom. Across continents
I've sown my seed, like Genghis Khan.
    Ancient Roman stinks, buried
deep in sewers and necromanced

    by rain, rose up to haunt our
kitchen sink until my roses
    washed us in perfume. Jasmine
petals pitched tents of scent over

    our terrace in Damascus.
And now in the Namib I nurse
    succulents, ungrateful as
actual children, who bristle

    truculently at my care,
resent their parent, and fail to
    thrive. I've adopted orphan
sprigs off starving plants. This one, from

    a burnt patch outside Tsumkwe,
grew on a spindle of sticks so

spare it made its eremic
kin look larded. Oryx browsed its

   twigs and I culled one, blithely
ignorant that its milk dripped on
      bare human skin would kindle
blisters faster than capsaicin.

   Lulled by its milder cousins'
suavity into casual
      potting protocol, I touched
my face and felt my cavalier

   behavior punished: a wee
Euphorbia damarana
      wants (my eyes aflame, mucus
membranes leaking) big caution. Aren't

   children awful? They morph us
into foreigners awkwardly
      inhabiting a country
whose customs we could not, once,

   have imagined enduring
even for a weekend. And though
      it's tough, we acclimatize;
soon we surprise ourselves serving

   the whims of tyrants we can't
not love. So. Here I cosset my
      lethal infant, pillowing
her in a bed of loamy sand,

trying to fathom how lit-
tle water I should offer in
        sips through the automated drip
system's nipple to keep the soil

        desiccated, almost. It's
a minimalist process, small
        as the infinitesimal
increments through which, from urban

        hoyden to doyenne of an
arid paradise, I have aged.
        Liquid seeps in so slowly
it dries before leaving its faint

        fingerprint under the urn.
Does it seem futile, my having
        raised blossoms for summers de-
cades of winters have razed? I've made

        nothing to outlive me, which
leaves me now with the luxury
        of time to smell each morning's
flowers while, yes, grieving rosebuds

        ungathered, etcetera.
I admit that, some days, alone
        among greenery, my roots in
this world feel very loose indeed.

        Though I know I'm needed: who
but me has time to feed moisture

with such attention through this
contraption? Likely not the San

mother lighting her pipe with
coal plucked from a blaze nourished by
    sticks off bushes I couldn't
identify. Self-sufficient,

    finding potable juices
in Tsama melons during droughts,
    her baby in a folded
envelope of hide hung over

    her shoulder (a letter to
herself in old age): our worlds seem
    so different. What might we have
in common besides our skin, which

    the hot wind wizens until
she soothes hers with !Nara oil and
    I grease mine with a store-bought
cream? I've heard it called a "spinster's

    pleasure," keeping a garden—
as if a fruitless woman must,
    at a certain age, nurture
part of nature she didn't let

    ripen in her; she's prone to
sour without this metonymic
    fecundity tamed by dis-
placement into the wet petal

and pistil glut with pollen.
But don't call it "simple" pleasure.
    It's an arduous ardor,
adoring the earth. Anyway,

    at a certain age even
simple pleasures are complex. Each
    day I tend my children, not
without whiffs of euphoria,

    but also sometimes with eyes
burning from all I've not touched, half-
    shut in sorrow, half in thanks,
half reverent, half hollowed out.

ACKNOWLEDGMENTS

My gratitude to the editors of journals where these poems first appeared:

Bennington Review: "Euphorbia"; *Ecotone*: "Some Say," "Elegy for Estrogen"; *Harvard Review*: "Africa Hand"; *Hopkins Review*: "Fado"; *Gettysburg Review*: "Ill-Starred"; *Gulf Coast*: "Sentimental Education"; *Missouri Review*: "Of Vinegar   Of Pearl" (sections 1–7); *Narrative*: "Animals & Instruments"; *New England Review*: "Gypsy Moths"; *Plume*: "A Gaze Hound That Hunteth by the Eye"; *Orion*: "Elegy for _____"; *32 Poems*: "Cliché," "Western Wind," "Wishes for Fifty"; *Tin House online*: "Orts & Slarts"; *Village Voice*: "The Soote Season"; *Zócalo Public Square*: "Blue Hour," "Call & Response."

Poetry Daily featured "Cliché" on April 8, 2023.

The Slowdown Show featured "Elegy for Estrogen" on November 12, 2021.

"Of Vinegar   Of Pearl" appeared as a chapbook from *Quarterly West* in May 2021.

I'm grateful for a 2019 Hawthornden Fellowship that allowed peace and decent ease to work on these poems.

Terrance Hayes, Nancy Krygowski, and Jeffrey McDaniel, thank you for your editorial enthusiasm. Many thanks also to Alex Wolfe, Joel W. Coggins, and Lesley Rains for turning a typescript into a beautiful object and sending it forth into the readers' hands.

Deborah Dancy, my gratitude for your vision and for sharing your art on the cover.

Thank you family, all my beloved in-laws and outlaws.

Grazie di cuore a Sabino Berardino, Nicole Cuddeback, Camille Dungy, Karen Holmberg, Shara McCallum, and Jane Satterfield for half a lifetime of sustaining conversations. Thank you Dana Shiller and Tom Marshall for letting me beak out with Lucy, the first best gaze hound. Thank you, Mark Rowe, for decades of nourishing letters and books and music, for your friendship and for reading my work with insight. For attention to this manuscript in its earlier incarnations, special thanks to Averill Curdy, Darcie Dennigan, Joshua Mehigan, Talia Neffson, and Christian Wiman.

Tony Deaton, you made me a home and then you gave me the world.